IQ Tests

To Keep You Sharp

Philip J. Carter
&
Kenneth A. Russell

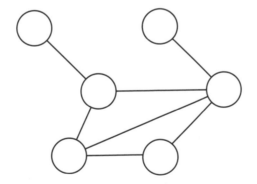

Sterling Publishing Co., Inc.
New York

Library of Congress Cataloging-in-Publication Data

Carter, Philip J.
IQ tests to keep you sharp / Philip J. Carter & Kenneth A. Russell.
  p. cm.
ISBN 0-8069-5789-1
1. Intelligence tests. 2. Self-evaluation. I. Russell, Kenneth A. II. Title.

BF431.3 .C363 2002
153.9'3–dc21   2001049215

Published by Sterling Publishing Co., Inc.
387 Park Avenue South, New York, N.Y. 10016
© 2002 by Philip J. Carter and Kenneth A. Russell
Distributed in Canada by Sterling Publishing
C/o Canadian Manda Group, 165 Dufferin Street,
Toronto, Ontario, Canada M6K 3H6
Distributed in Great Britain by Chrysalis Books
64 Brewery Road, London N7 9NT England
Distributed in Australia by Capricorn Link (Australia) Pty. Ltd.
P.O. Box 704, Windsor, NSW 2756 Australia
10 9 8 7 6 5
Manufactured in China
All rights reserved

Sterling ISBN 0-8069-5789-1

For information about custom editions, special sales,
premium and corporate purchases, please contact Sterling
Special Sales Department at 800-805-5489 or
specialsales@sterlingpub.com

Contents

Multidiscipline Tests

Introduction

The tests in this book are specially compiled to provide fun and entertainment to those who take them. At the same time, the questions are designed to be similar in format to those you are likely to encounter in IQ tests. If you perform well on these tests you are likely to do well on actual IQ tests. Because they have been specially compiled for this publication, the tests are not standardized and, therefore, an actual IQ score cannot be given. Nevertheless, we do provide an approximate guide to performance on each test, for those of you who may wish to exercise your competitive instincts. We also provide a time limit for those of you wishing to try the tests against the clock.

An IQ test usually consists of several different types of questions. These are basically verbal, numerical, visual (culture fair), and logic. To help you test yourself in each of these disciplines separately, and identify individual strengths and possible weaknesses which need to be worked on, we have arranged the tests in the book into five sections: verbal, visual, numerical, calculation and logic, and multidiscipline. The verbal, numerical, and calculation and logic sections consist of five individual tests with fifteen questions in each test. The visual section consists of three tests with fifteen questions each. The final section, multidiscipline, which brings together all the four types of questions in the previous sections, consists of five individual tests with twenty questions in each test.

Scoring chart per test (each correct answer scores 1 point):

Sections 1–4 (verbal, visual, numerical*, calculation and logic)

15	Genius level
14	Mastermind
13	Exceptional
11–12	Excellent
9–10	Very good
7–8	Good
5–6	Average

Time limit: 40 minutes per test

Section 5 (multidiscipline)

20	Genius level
18–19	Mastermind
16–17	Exceptional
14–15	Excellent
12–13	Very good
10–11	Good
8–9	Average

Time limit: 60 minutes per test.

*Calculators may be used for these questions. It will not invalidate your score.

Verbal

1. Complete the six words so that the same two letters that end the first word start the second and the same two letters that end the second start the third word, etc. The same two letters that end the sixth word start the first word to complete the circle.

SI MI LE
LE AS ED
ED SI DE
DE FI NE
NE NG ED
ED RE SE

2. My energy is such that an oscillatory motion is taking place within my every roller-shaped chamber caused by the ignition of an explosive mixture. What am I doing?

3. CELEBRATE TEA-RIOT is an anagram of which two words that are ten-letters and six-letters long and opposite in meaning?

4. "An indirect, ingenious, and often cunning means to gain an end." What word fits closest to this definition?

SHENANIGAN, ARTIFICE, SUBTERFUGE, PLOT, SOPHISM

5. Work from letter to letter horizontally, vertically, or diagonally to spell out a seventeen-letter phrase.

LIFT LIFE TORN
HATE

L	I	A		
K	F	T		
E	H	E	O	N
		S	R	I
		E	K	L

6. Which two words are closest in meaning?

LOYAL, GRACIOUS, CONFIDENT, SALUBRIOUS, CORDIAL, COMELY

7. Place a word in the parentheses so that it makes a new word, phrase, or hyphenated word when added to the end of the first word, and makes another new word, phrase, or hyphenated word when placed in front of the second word.

CANNON (_BALL_) BEARINGS

8. Join three of the two-letter groups together to make a six-letter word that is a TREE.

IA, AC, CA, IN, AC, TK, PI, NA

9. Which word means the same as ERUBESCENT?

CHUBBY, BLUSHING, SPOTTY, CHARMING, JEALOUS, ENVIOUS

10. Which five-letter word can be placed at the end of these six words to make new words or phrases?

CLUB
DOLL
GREEN
FULL   (_HOUSE_)
SAFE
PENT

11. Find a six-letter word using only these five letters.

W   G

    I   WIGGLE

L   E

12. What is the longest word that you can find by moving from square to square and only using each letter once? The answer is a ten-letter word.

A	N	C	E	K
F	M	G	S	T
O	G	Y	B	I
D	U	L	V	H
S	P	E	J	X

13. Complete the three-letter words to make an eight-letter word on the bottom line.

S	E	A	A	C	E	A	A
O	R	S	S	U	G	D	R

14. Fill in the blanks to make two eight-letter words that are synonyms. You can go clockwise or counterclockwise.

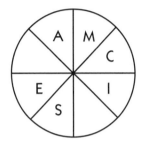

15. Find the starting point and track from letter to letter along the lines to find the name of a country (5,3,6).

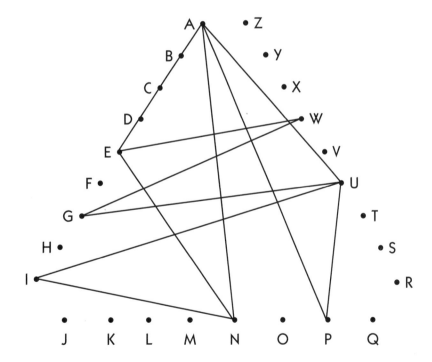

Verbal

1. Which word is the most opposite in meaning to PITHY?

MERCIFUL, ABJECT, LOQUACIOUS,

COMICAL, SUCCINCT, EXPLICIT

2. Which word will fit in front of these words to make new words?

OWED
EAR
(_ _ _) LESS
LONG
ANGER

3. Read clockwise to figure out this sixteen-letter word. Only alternate letters are shown, and you have to find the starting point.

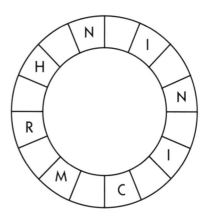

4. Which word is the odd one out?

DECODE, TRANSLATE, ENCIPHER,

INTERPRET, REVEAL

5. Move a word from the right-hand column to the words in the left-hand column.

CAP   BOOK
MARE   DREAM
OWL   GOWN
SHADE   BREAK
?

6. Add one letter, not necessarily the same letter, to each word in the front, end, or middle to find two words that are similar in meaning.

NICE   LACE

7. Change just one letter in each of the four words to spell out a familiar phrase.

SEAL   LINE   HIT   CARES

8. Find two words which mean the opposite.

MALADROIT, DEXTROUS, IGNOMINY, NECESSARY, STUPEFY, MODERATION

9. Join two of the four-letter groups together to make an eight-letter word which is an ANIMAL.

MAND, CHIN, RILE, TIGE, CAPU, CHIL

10. What is the name given to a group of EAGLES?

(a) SIMPLICITY   (b) HILL   (c) CONVOCATION   (d) DRAUGHT   (e) PLUMP

11. Take one letter from each animal (in order) to make another animal.

POSSUM
DONKEY
ERMINE
KITTEN
RHESUS
CAYMAN

12. Which word will fit in front of these words to make new words or phrases?

(_ _ _ _)

CAKE
BOWL
HOOK
KNIFE
NET
TAIL

13. The vowels A, E, I, O, and U have been removed from this trite saying. See if you can replace them.

NYNWH   THNKS   THRSS   MGDNV   RYNHS

NTNTR   VWDNG   HPPL

14. Find a nine-letter word by starting at a corner and spiraling to the center.

G	U	T
N	N	A
A	R	O

15. Fill in the blanks to find an eight-letter word. You can go clockwise or counterclockwise.

Verbal

1. Which two words are the most opposite in meaning?

    AMBIGUOUS, NECESSARY, DESTITUTE,
    INEVITABLE, SUPERFLUOUS, UNUSUAL

2. Place the letters in the correct boxes in each quadrant to obtain two eight-letter words, one reading clockwise and the other counterclockwise. The two words are antonyms.

    NE: ENNP
    SE: ORAN
    SW: IPPT
    NW: STOA

3. PRONGHORN : ANTELOPE
    HELLBENDER :

    (a) SNAKE   (b) COUGAR   (c) SALAMANDER
    (d) SPIDER   (e) STICKLEBACK

4. With the aid of the clue below, find two words that form a palindrome, i.e., a phrase that reads the same backwards and forwards. For example: HIGHEST BILLING = TOP SPOT.

    WICKED FRUIT

5. What is the longest word in the English language that can be produced from the following ten letters?

    ACEIMNORVW

6. Place two letters in each pair of words so that they finish the word on the left and start the word on the right. The letters in the parentheses reading in pairs downwards will spell out an eight-letter word.

RI (_ _) AR
CO (_ _) ER
LA (_ _) AR
OV (_ _) LY

7. Make a six-letter word using only these four letters.

E   R
U   D

8. Which word means the opposite of NEGATION?

(a) DEBATABLE   (b) MOROSE   (c) INFLUENCE
(d) AFFIRMATION   (e) MUSTINESS

9. Join two of the three-letter groups together to make a six-letter word which is an HERB.

RET, VES, GAR, SOR, CHI, LIK

10. Complete the word.

_ _ UBRE _ _ _

Clue: Found on the stage

11. Rearrange these words to make a trite saying.

MIDDLE	THAN	FAT	MENACED
FAT	THE	BY	IT
AROUND	THE	SOCIETY	IS
IS	THE	LESS	EARS
THREATENED	THE	BY	BETWEEN

12. Fill in the blanks to find two words which are antonyms. You can go clockwise or counterclockwise.

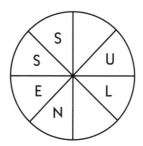

13. Add one letter, not necessarily the same letter, to these words to find six new words all on the same theme.

CAP, CAB, ACE, CHB, NET

14. What is the longest word that you can find by moving from square to square and only using each letter once? The answer is a ten-letter word.

B	J	N	Q	U
A	T	E	W	F
M	D	H	P	X
R	I	G	Y	O
V	L	K	S	C

15. Find two sports by placing the letters in the squares.

E   C   F
E   G   I
I   K   N
N   R   T

Verbal

1. Only one set of letters below can be arranged into a five-letter English word. Can you find the word?

   N U T R P
   E B N P L
   O G P N E
   H I R C T
   S A B T L
   U N T G E
   M U R D O
   E N T U C
   M N T E L
   E P L O N

2. Which word comes closest in meaning to PROSAIC?

   DELIBERATE, BANAL, ANCIENT, UNUSUAL, DISCORDANT

3. Only ten letters of the alphabet do not appear in the array below. What ten-letter phrase can be spelled out from the missing letters?

W	M	Y	J
G	Z	O	Q
K	T	F	N
P	X	L	H

   Clue: Might this person occasionally get that sinking feeling?

4. A quotation by Louis Pasteur has been split into three-letter groups which have then been arranged into random order. Can you put the letters in the correct order and reveal the quotation?

   PRE, ORS, IND, CHA, THE, EDM, FAV, PAR, NCE

5. Working clockwise, take one letter from each circle in turn to spell out two synonyms.

Clue: Each word starts in a different circle.

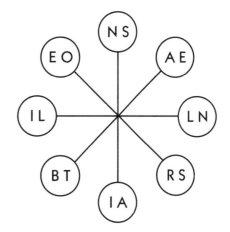

6. RATTLE PUFFY MICE is an anagram of which two words that are similar in meaning (6,9)?

7. Start at one of the corner squares and spiral clockwise to the center letter to spell out a nine-letter word. You have to provide the missing letters.

	L	
I	E	L
S	U	A

8. The vowels A, E, I, O, and U have been omitted from this trite saying. See if you can replace them.

THWRL   DGTSB   TTRVR   YDYTH   NWRSG   NNTHV   NNG

9. Which two words are the closest in meaning?

PERMEATED, OBSTINATE, CORPOREAL, TRIFLING, PRODIGIOUS, DOGGED

10. What is a CARAPACE?

(a) A SHELL   (b) A BODKIN   (c) A MIDGET

(d) A HAYSTACK   (e) A MEASURE

11. Join three sets of the three letters to make two nine-letter words.

SEC, ECT, RET, IVE, INV, ION

12. Which word means the opposite of SABLE?

(a) AWKWARD
(b) BURDEN
(c) ACUTE
(d) BLACK
(e) WHITE

13. Fill in the blanks to find two eight-letter words which are synonyms. You can go clockwise or counterclockwise.

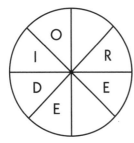 

14. Complete the three-letter words to make an eight-letter word in the bottom line.

A	E	A	H	S	A	E	W
S	M	S	I	K	R	R	I

15. Find an eight-letter word by filling in the blanks. You can go clockwise or counter-clockwise.

Verbal

1. Six synonyms of the word PARTNER are shown. Take one letter from each of the synonyms (in order) to find another synonym of PARTNER.

   ASSOCIATE, SPOUSE, COMPANION, HUSBAND, COLLEAGUE, COMRADE, MATE

2. If meat in a river is T(HAM)ES, can you find a brave man in a Native American tribe?

3. Insert a word in the parentheses that means the same as the definitions outside the parentheses.

   Barred frame (   ) Grind noisily

4. Find four six-letter words with the aid of the clues. The same three letters in each word are represented by XYZ, which is a familiar three-letter word.

X Y Z _ _ _	Overthrow
_ X Y Z _ _	A place of ideal perfection
_ _ X Y Z _	Prevents
_ _ _ X Y Z	Type of computer

5. Insert an American city into the bottom line to complete the nine three-letter words.

F	T	A	A	P	W	P	R	B
I	O	R	S	I	A	A	U	A

6. Use each letter of this newspaper headline only once to spell out three kinds of precious minerals.

   LAZY ATTEMPTS - OH DEAR ME!

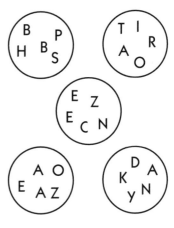

7. Take one letter from each circle in turn to spell out five foods.

8. Place a word in the parentheses which means the same as the two words outside the parentheses.

ASSISTANT (_ _ _ _ _ _) RUNNER-UP

9. Find a one-word anagram for DREAM LILT.

10. Put four out of these five two-letter groups together to make an eight-letter fish.

OU   ER   AI   ND   FL

11. Find a nine-letter word using only these four letters.

N A
S I

12. Fill in the blanks to find two eight-letter words which are synonyms. You can go clockwise or counterclockwise.

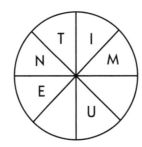

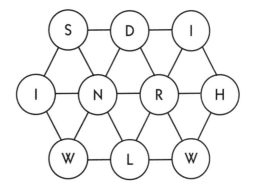

13. Spell out a ten-letter word by moving into each circle only once.

Clue: Inclement weather

14. Rearrange these boxes to make a trite saying.

WORMS	TO	A	ONLY
ONCE	TO	USE	THE
OF	RECAN	CAN	A
YOU	CAN	CAN	THEM
OPEN	IS	WAY	LONGER

15. Fill in the blanks to find a ten-letter word. You can go clockwise or counterclockwise.

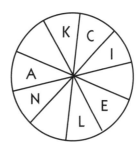

Visual

1. What comes next in the sequence?

   ?

A.   **B.**   **C.**   **D.**   **E.**

2. is to

as

 is to

A.   **B.**   **C.**   **D.**   **E.**   **F.**

3. Which is the odd one out?

A.   **B.**   **C.**

D.   **E.**   **F.**

4.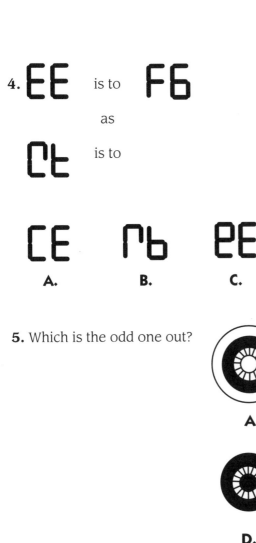

5. Which is the odd one out?

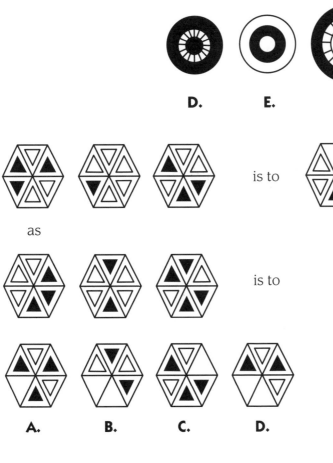

6.

7. Which symbol is missing from the circle?

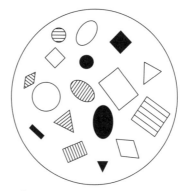

 A.   B.   C.   D.   E.

8. What comes next in the sequence?

 A.   B.   C.   D.   E.

9. Which is the odd one out?

A. B. C. D.

E. F. G.

10.

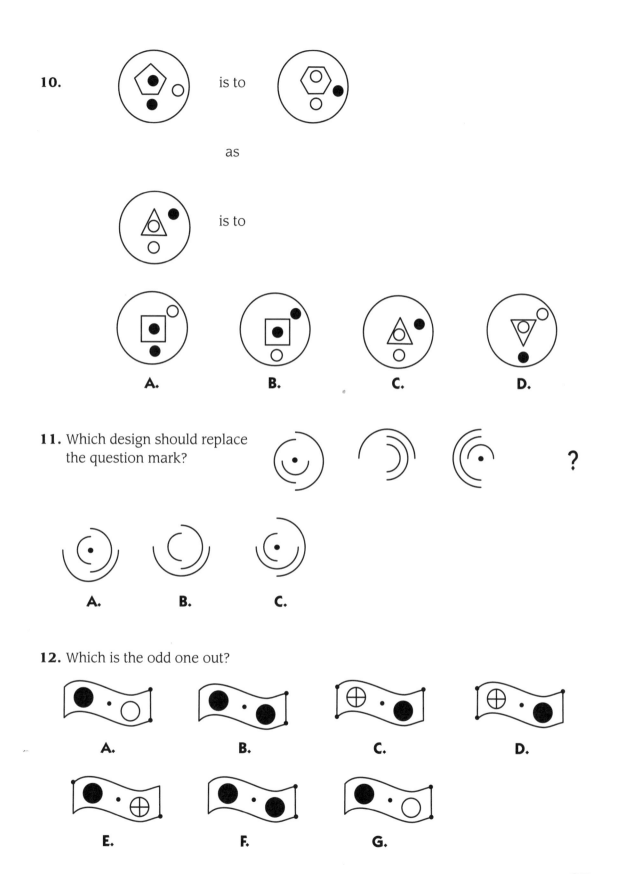

is to

as

is to

A.　　B.　　C.　　D.

11. Which design should replace the question mark?

?

A.　　B.　　C.

12. Which is the odd one out?

A.　　B.　　C.　　D.

E.　　F.　　G.

13.

What comes next in the above sequence?

A.   **B.**   **C.**   **D.**   **E.**

14. What is the total of the numbers on the reverse side of these dice?

15. What is the average area of the 7 shapes in square units?

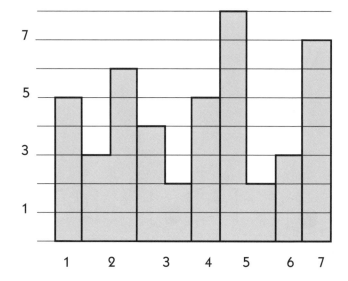

Visual

1.  is to

as

 is to

A.   B.   C.   D.   E.

2.

                  ?

What comes next in the above sequence?

A.   B.   C.   D.   E.

A.   B.   C.   D.   E.

3. Which is the odd one out?

A.   B.   C.   D.   E.

4. What comes next in the sequence?

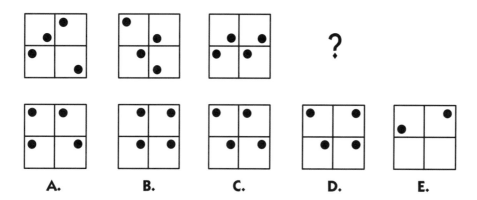

A. B. C. D. E.

5. Which square should replace the question mark?

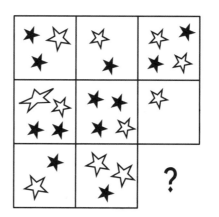

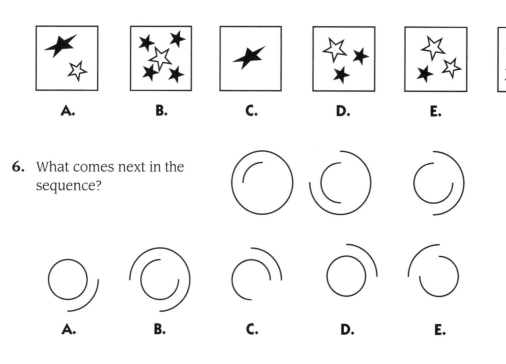

A. B. C. D. E. F.

6. What comes next in the sequence?

A. B. C. D. E.

7. The contents of which shield below are most like the contents of the shield to the right?

A.   **B.**   **C.**   **D.**   **E.**

8. Which is the odd one out?

 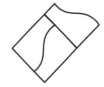

A.   **B.**   **C.**

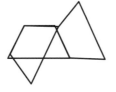 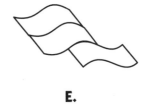 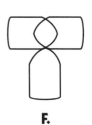

D.   **E.**   **F.**

9.

 is to as is to

A.   **B.**   **C.**   **D.**

10. If &*+# is to +#&*

Then +>#= is to ?

A. =>+#   **B.** #=+>   **C.** #+>=   **D.** =>+#

11. Which is the odd one out?

A.   **B.**   **C.**

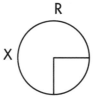   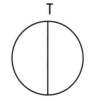

D.   **E.**   **F.**   **G.**

R   S   T

X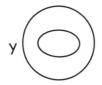

12. Which circle should replace the
question mark?

y

z ?

A.   **B.**   **C.**   **D.**   **E.**

13. Each line and symbol that appears in the four outer circles above is transferred to the center circle according to these rules:

If a line or symbol occurs in the outer circles:

once, then it is transferred.
twice, then it is possibly transferred.
three times, then it is transferred.
four times, then it is not transferred.

Which of the circles A, B, C, D, or E shown below should appear at the center of the diagram above?

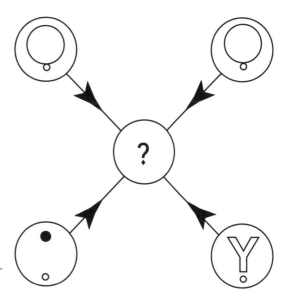

A.   **B.**   **C.**   **D.**   **E.**

14. Which is the odd one out?

A.   **B.**   **C.**   **D.**   **E.**   **F.**   **G.**

15. What is the total value of these three angles?

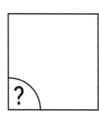 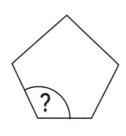 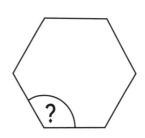

A.   **B.**   **C.**

Visual

1. Which is the odd one out?

    A.   **B.**   **C.**   **D.**   **E.**

2. is to

           A.   **B.**   **C.**

    as

 is to

           D.   **E.**

3. How many lines appear at the right?

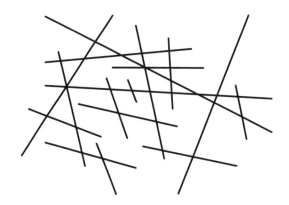

4. Which is the odd one out?

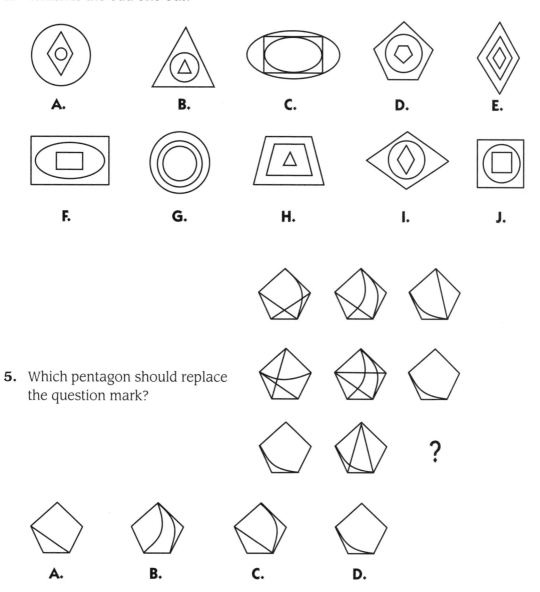

5. Which pentagon should replace the question mark?

6. Which is the odd one out?

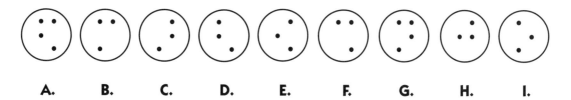

7. To which of the squares below can a dot be added so that the dot then meets the same conditions as the dot in the square to the right?

A.   **B.**   **C.**   **D.**   **E.**

8. Which hexagon should replace the question mark?

A.   **B.**   **C.**   **D.**   **E.**

9. Which is the odd one out?

A.   **B.**   **C.**   **D.**

E.   **F.**   **G.**

10.  is to 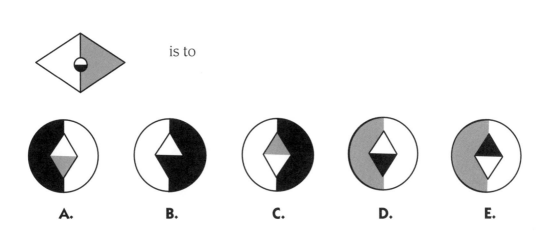 as

 is to

A.   **B.**   **C.**   **D.**   **E.**

11. Each line and symbol that appears in the four outer circles is transferred to the center circle according to these rules:

If a line or symbol occurs in the outer circles:

once, then it is transferred.
twice, then it is possibly transferred.
three times, then it is transferred.
four times, then it is not transferred.

Which of the circles A, B, C, D, or E shown below should appear at the center of the diagram above?

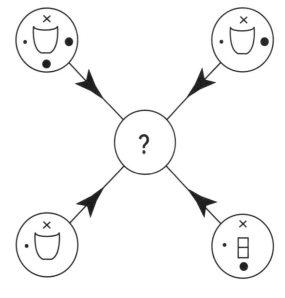

A.   **B.**   **C.**   **D.**   **E.**

12. Each pair of circles produces the circle above by carrying forward only those elements that are different. Similar elements are canceled out. Which circle should replace the question mark?

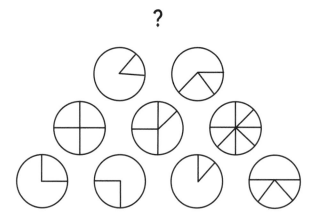

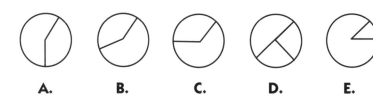

A.   **B.**   **C.**   **D.**   **E.**

13. Each of the nine squares in the grid marked 1A to 3C should incorporate all the lines and symbols which are shown in the squares of the same letter and number immediately above and to the left. For example, 2B should incorporate all the lines and symbols that are in 2 and B.

One of the squares is incorrect. Which one is it?

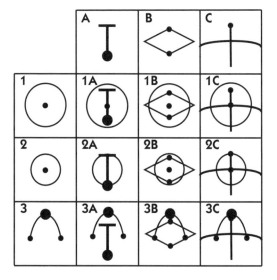

14. Which symbol should replace the question mark?

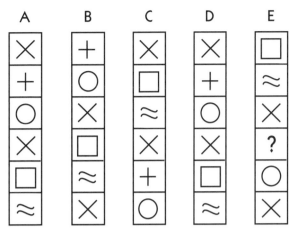

15. Which circle should replace the question mark?

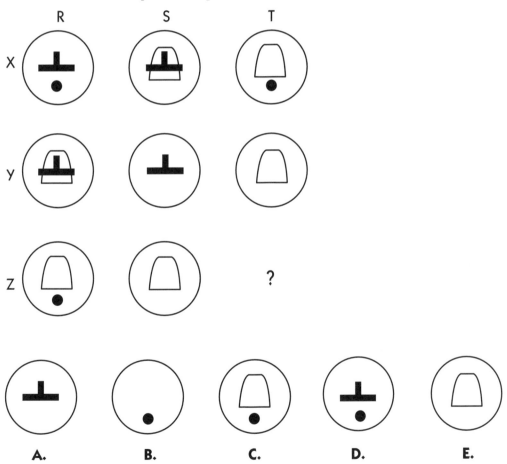

Numerical

1. What number should replace the question mark?

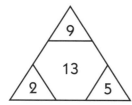 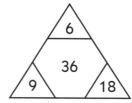 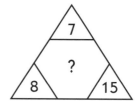

2. What number comes next in the sequence below ?

3624, 4363, 3644, 4563, 3664, ?

3. What number should replace the question mark?

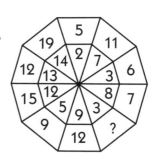

4. What four digits should appear in the middle section?

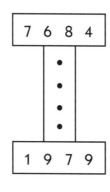

5. What number should replace the question mark?

```
    2              4              ?
  7 4 4        6 9 5          3 8 6
```

6. Each line of numbers follows the same logical progression. Replace the question marks with the correct numbers.

3 8 2 4	1 1 6	?
4 9 6 8	?	1 8
7 5 1 9	?	?

7. Which number is the odd one out?

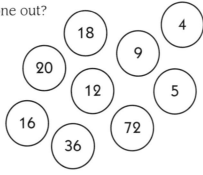

8. A man caught a fish. It weighed $\frac{5}{7}$ kg + $\frac{5}{7}$ its own weight. What did it weigh?

9. What number should replace the question mark?

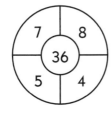 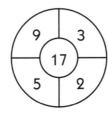 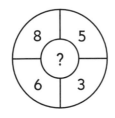

10. What fraction will produce this recurring decimal?

.166166166....

11. Which number should replace the question mark?

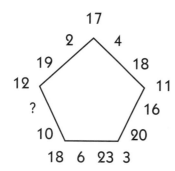

17

2　4

19　18

12　11

?　16

10　20

18　6　23　3

12. What number should replace the question mark?

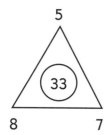 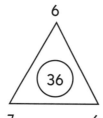 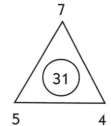 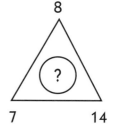

5　　6　　7　　8

33　36　31　?

8　7　7　6　5　4　7　14

13. What number should replace the question mark?

4	2	9	8	6
3	8	7	9	5
8	1	7	?	1

14. What number comes next?

0, 1, 3, 6, 7, 9, 12, 13, ?

15. What number should replace the question mark?

8	9	3	69
7	5	6	29
4	7	9	19
9	8	4	?

Numerical

1. Multiply by 7 the number of odd numbers that are immediately followed by an even number in the row of numbers below. What is the answer?

   4 2 8 7 5 3 2 5 1 7 4 6 8 1 4 2 5 7 6 8 3 1 9

2. What number is two places away from itself less 3, two places away from itself plus 2, two places away from itself plus 4, three places away from itself less 1, and three places away from itself less 5?

10	24	1	27	9
2	11	5	7	3
29	16	25	12	18
17	14	8	4	13
9	20	22	6	15

3. What number should replace the question mark?

4. What number should replace the question mark?

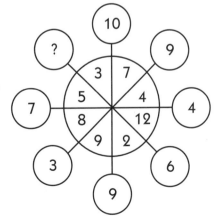

5. What number should replace the question mark?

2836 : 13
9423 : 14
7229 : ?

6. What number should replace the question mark?

7	4	5	3
1	6	3	7
3	8	1	7
6	1	8	?

7. What number should replace the question mark?

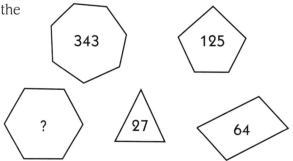

8. The average of three numbers is 24.
The average of two numbers of these three numbers is 22½.
What is the value of the third number?

9. If a test score goes up 15% from x to 69, what was the previous test score?

10. What number should replace the question mark?

27, 27, 30¼, 23¾, 33½, 20½, 36¾, 17¼, ?

11. What number should replace the question mark?

39	3	4	9
54	6	8	6
45	36	9	1
35	7	7	?

12. What number should replace the question mark?

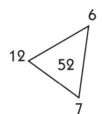 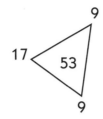 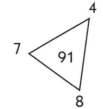 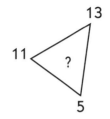

13. What number should replace the question mark?

1st	2nd	3rd	4th
26	27	29	25
28	29	31	36
30	31	37	49
32	33	?	64
34	35	43	81

14. Which is the odd one out?

16   36   64   27   81

A.   B.   C.   D.   E.

15. What number should replace the question mark ?

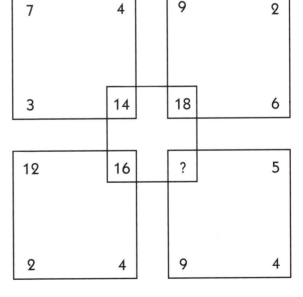

Numerical

1. 6, 50, 402, 3218, ?

What number comes next in the above sequence?

2. What number should replace the question mark?

3. What number should replace the question mark?

4. What number should replace the question mark?

		8		6		
	3		8		7	
5		4		8		5
2		9		4		7
	?		5		4	
		5		9		

5. What number should replace the question mark?

4322 : 48
4172 : 56
7615 : ?

6. What number should replace the question mark?

7. Which two numbers, one in the top rectangle and one in the bottom rectangle, are the odd ones out?

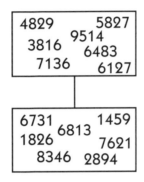

8. Find the value of x:

$$(16)(3^2) = (2^3)x$$

9. Simplify

$$(87^2) - (86^2).$$

10. What number should replace the question mark?

17	26	21	30
38	29	34	25
33	42	37	?

11.

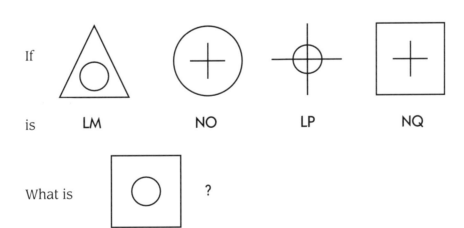

If △(with circle) is LM ⊕(circle with cross) is NO ϕ(cross with circle) is LP ⊡(square with cross) is NQ

What is ☐(square with circle) ?

12. What number should replace the question mark?

7	12	9

13	18	15

11	16	13

17	22	?

13. What number should replace the question mark?

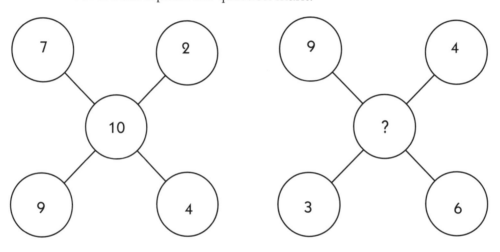

14. What number should replace the question mark?

42	7	6	12
91	13	4	11
88	11	5	13
27	9	8	?

15. What number should replace the question mark?

16		23		28		38		?

Numerical

1. What number should replace the question mark?

27 ⊃⊂ 146 ⊃⊂ 42

39 ⊃⊂ 548 ⊃⊂ 56

17 ⊃⊂ ? ⊃⊂ 13

2. What number should replace the question mark?

```
?
5   3
3   3   1
2   1   2   1
1   1   1   1   1
```

3. What number should replace the question mark?

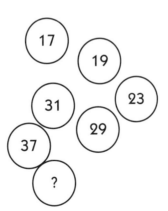

17
19
31   23
29
37
?

4. What number should replace the question mark?

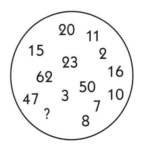

20 11
15   2
23
62   16
47   3 50 10
?   7
8

5. These numbers are in logical groupings. What number should replace the question mark?

7		5		6	
8	3	7	5	?	6
2	9	1	5	1	6

6. What numbers should appear on the bottom row?

2	4	3	7	11
10	5	13	9	7
22	23	17	19	18
?	?	?	?	?

7. Simplify and find the value for x:

$$X = \cfrac{1}{\cfrac{2}{3} - \cfrac{1}{2}}$$

8. What fraction will produce this recurring decimal?

.71288888888888 . . .

9. What should replace the question mark?

82, 82, 86¼, 77¾, 90½, 73½, 94¾, 69¼, ?

10. Simplify to find the value of x:

x = (−5) − (−7) − (−2)

11. What is the value of the angle in an octagon?

12. What number should replace the question mark?

6	7	4	52
8	5	3	39
4	3	8	56
5	2	4	?

13. What number should replace the question mark?

14. What value weight should be placed at the question mark to balance the scale?

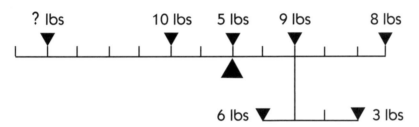

15.

KL   MN   KP   MQ   KQ

What is the code for this symbol ?

Numerical

1. What number comes next?

7, 12, 20, 34, 60, ?

2. What number should replace the question mark?

7	4	3	25
6	2	4	8
7	8	5	51
3	9	8	?

3. Which of these numbers is the odd one out?

2446

8429

2137

3248

6379

2483

1226

5687

4. Multiply the third-highest odd number in the left-hand group with the third-lowest even number in the right-hand group. What is the answer?

37	42	96	44	23		46	59	56	89	18
64	35	21	39	59		69	52	50	11	72
56	31	78	58	16		37	15	68	92	25
26	47	34	74	29		51	44	19	82	54
66	33	84	27	68		48	11	27	26	21

5. What number should replace the question mark?

45 (2) 52
97 (7) 33
67 (?) 72

6. What number comes next?

1, 1, 3, 6, 5, 11, 7, ?

7. What number should replace the question mark?

4812 : 72
7324 : 13
9417 : ?

8. What number should replace the question mark?

| 60 | 78 | 82 | 102 | 93 | 115 | 106 | ? |

9. What number should replace the question mark?

7   15   34   71   ?

10. What number should replace the question mark?

13
76   19
17   68
52

42
16   11
66   7
96

21
14   19
?   126
189

11. What number should replace the question mark?

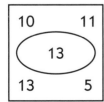 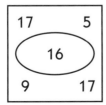 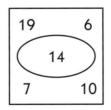 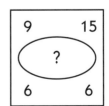

10	11	17	5	19	6	9	15
13		16		14		?	
13	5	9	17	7	10	6	6

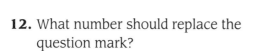

12. What number should replace the question mark?

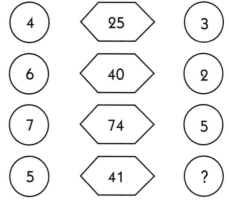

13. What number should replace the question mark?

172   468   317   246   ?

14. Simplify

$^{17}/_{19} \div {}^{68}/_{38} \div {}^{16}/_{32}.$

15. Place the correct numbers in the vacant pyramid bricks.

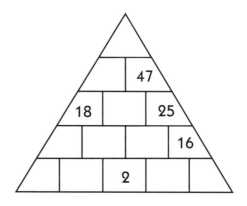

Each brick is the total of the two bricks that are supporting it. (One number is –6.)

Calculation and Logic

1. What letter is two to the right of the letter immediately to the left of the letter three to the right of the letter C?

   A B C D E F G H

2. How many minutes is it before 12 noon if 55 minutes ago it was four times as many minutes past 8 AM as it is minutes before noon now?

3. Sid is one-and-a-half times as old as Alf who is one-and-a-half times as old as Jim. Their combined ages total 133. How old are the three men?

4. The following words are in a logical progression:

   PAINT
   UMPIRE
   FANATIC
   DARKNESS

   Which word comes next?

   ABDICATED, TRUCULENT, GARDENING, THROUGHOUT, CHIEFTAIN, ARILLODE

5. If five lemons and two oranges cost $4.60 and two lemons and three oranges cost $3.60, what is the cost of an orange and what is the cost of a lemon?

6. My watch showed the correct time at 12 noon, but then the battery started to run down until it eventually stopped completely. Between 12 noon up to its stopping, it lost 15 minutes per hour on average. It now shows 6 PM, but it stopped 3 hours ago. What is the correct time now?

7. You have picked 667 apples from the trees in your orchard, which you are putting into bags to give your neighbors. You wish to put an equal number of apples into each bag, and you wish to use as few bags as possible. How many apples should you put into how many bags?

8. A number plus ²⁄₅ of that number, plus 6, minus 4¹⁄₂₅ is 3²⁄₂₅. What is the number?

9. How do you change Celsius to Fahrenheit and vice versa?

10. An assistant was slicing bacon. He sliced each slab of bacon into 16 slices at the rate of 60 slices per minute. How many slabs had he chopped up after 20 minutes?

11. Two square floors had to be covered in 12-in. tiles. The number of tiles used was 850. Each side of one floor was 10 ft. more than the other floor. What were the dimensions of the two floors?

12. In 9 years' time the combined age of my four brothers will be 99. What will it be in 11 years' time?

13. Which is the odd one out?

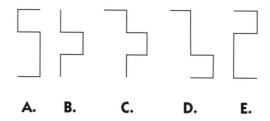

A.   B.   C.   D.   E.

14. At the boarding school, three sisters travel home regularly. One travels every 5 days, one travels every 6 days, and one travels every 7 days. When will they all return to the school at the same time?

15. Five friends live in street-corner buildings in New York City. Where should they meet in order to cut down their walking time to a minimum?

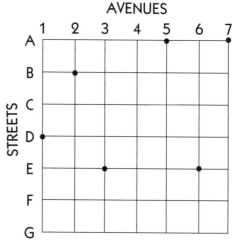

Calculation and Logic

1. Al beats Bill at chess but loses to Hillary. Chelsea usually wins against Bill but never against Hillary. Who is the weakest player?

2. What comes next in the sequence?

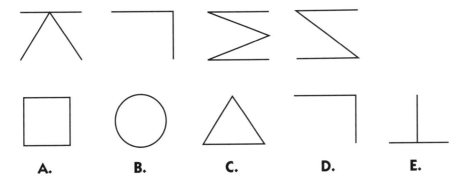

   A.   B.   C.   D.   E.

3. FINAL (FLIRT) ENTER

   Using the same logic as in the example above, what word is coded to appear in the bracket below?

   BIKER (_ _ _ _ _) RIFLE

4. A train traveling at a speed of 75 mph enters a tunnel 1.25 miles long. The length of the train is 0.25 miles. How long does it take for all of the train to pass through the tunnel, from the moment the front enters to the moment the rear emerges?

5. If a man weighs 75% of his own weight plus 42 lbs, how much does he weigh?

6. Frasier had twice as many as Niles, and Niles had twice as many as Daphne. But then Daphne lost one of hers, and of the ones she then had left, she gave twice as many to Frasier as she gave to Niles. This meant that Frasier still had less than 20, but still had twice as many as Niles.

   How many did each have originally?

7. These clocks follow a weird kind of logic. What time should the fourth clock face show?

   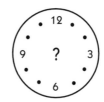

8. The dog and kennel cost more than $20. If the dog had cost $5 more, the kennel would have cost ⅓ of the total. If the kennel had cost $5 less, I would have spent ¾ of the total on the dog.

What was the cost of the dog?

9. A large square had an area of 490 sq ft. It was the same area as two smaller squares. One had a side that was 3 times the length of the other.

What were the areas of the two smaller squares?

10. Ten people shared a birthday cake. They all had equal portions and yet one piece remained on the plate.

How was this possible?

11. Replace the letters with numbers so that the sum is correct.

```
  S L O W
  S L O W
+   O L D
─────────
  OW L S
```

12. I had a 99-year lease; ⅔ of the time past was equal to ⅘ of the time to come.

How much of the lease had expired?

13. The combined ages of:
Alice and Barbara is 76.
Alice and Chloe is 96.
Barbara and Chloe is 140.
How old are Alice, Barbara, and Chloe?

14. Find the weight to balance the scale.

15. Four cheeses of different sizes are placed on Stool A. How many moves will it take to move the cheeses one by one to Stool C? A cheese must not be placed on a cheese smaller than itself.

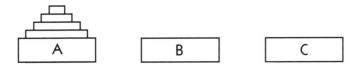

Calculation and Logic

1. Jack and Jill share their sweets in the ratio of 3:8. If Jill has 56 sweets, how many does Jack have?

2. You are trying to fill your bathtub with both hot and cold water, but you accidentally forgot to put the stopper in the drain. The hot tap takes 4.5 minutes to fill the bath. The cold tap takes 12 minutes to fill the bath. The plug hole takes 18 minutes to empty a full bath.

   How long will it take for the bath to fill completely?

3. In my wardrobe all but four of my jackets are brown, all but four are blue, all but four are gray, all but four are green, and all but four are black. How many jackets do I have altogether?

4. Your boss offers you a choice of two options by which your new salary is to be calculated.

   First option: Initial salary $40,000 to be increased after each 12 months by $2000.

   Second option: Initial salary $40,000 to be increased after each 6 months by $500.

   The salary will be calculated every six months.

   Which option should you choose?

5. Four playing cards are placed in a row. The King of Hearts is next to the Ace of Spades, but not next to the Three of Diamonds. The Three of Diamonds is not next to the Nine of Clubs. Which card is next to the Nine of Clubs?

6. Between fifty and a hundred people hired a private carriage for a railway trip. They paid a total of $2847. Each person paid the same amount, which was an exact number of dollars. How many people went on the trip?

7. There are a number of lions and eagles at the zoo. In all, they have 30 heads and 86 legs. How many lions and how many eagles are there?

8. Which day is two days after the day four days before the day immediately following the day two days before Saturday?

SUNDAY
MONDAY
TUESDAY
WEDNESDAY
THURSDAY
FRIDAY
SATURDAY

9. My friend lives on a long road where the numbers of the houses run consecutively from 1 to 82. To find his number, I asked him three questions to which I received either a "yes" or "no" answer to each. The questions were:

1. Is it under 41?
2. Is it divisible by 4?
3. Is it a square number?

My friend answered "yes" twice and "no" once. From my friend's answers, I was able to determine for certain what the house number was. What is the house number?

10. At a golf club, Man A challenged Man B to a match. Man A scored 72, Man B scored 69. Man A won, but it was not match play. How was that possible?

11. I am thinking of a number between 99 and 999.

1. The number is below 500.
2. It is a square number.
3. It is a cube number.
4. The first and last digits are 5, 7, or 9.

One of the first three statements is a lie. What is the number?

12. I asked my son to tell me how many stamps he had. He replied, "The number if divided by 2 will give a remainder of 1, divided by 3 a remainder of 2, by 4 a remainder of 3, by 5 a remainder of 4, by 6 a remainder of 5, by 7 a remainder of 6, by 8 a remainder of 7, by 9 a remainder of 8, by 10 a remainder of 9."

How many stamps did he have, if he had fewer than 5,000 stamps?

13. Arthur and Bert built the brickwork of a house in 24 days. If Arthur can do only two-thirds as much as Bert, how long would it take each of them working alone?

14. Replace the letters with numbers so that the product is correct.

$$
\begin{array}{r}
\text{W H A T} \\
\times \quad \text{A} \\
\hline
\text{S H O W}
\end{array}
$$

15. A man left a sum of money to his three children. Albert is to get 20% more than Jasper and 25% more than Cyril. Jasper's share is $3600. How much does Cyril get?

Calculation and Logic

1. Insert the numbers 1 to 6 into the circles so that for any particular circle the sum of numbers in the circles connected directly to it equals the value corresponding to the number, as given in the list.

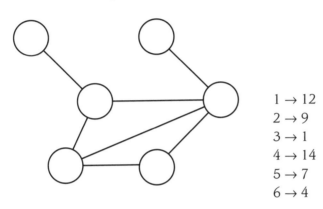

1 → 12
2 → 9
3 → 1
4 → 14
5 → 7
6 → 4

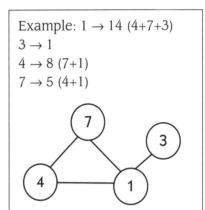

Example: 1 → 14 (4+7+3)
3 → 1
4 → 8 (7+1)
7 → 5 (4+1)

2. A man has 47 colored socks in his drawer: 14 identical blue socks, 23 identical red socks, and 10 identical gray. The lights have failed and he is left completely in the dark. How many socks must he take out of the drawer to be 100% certain he has at least one pair of each color?

3. In a game with 24 players that lasts for exactly 50 minutes, there are 24 players plus 8 reserves who alternate equally with each player. This means that all players, including reserves, are on the field for the same length of time. How long is that?

4. What number comes next?

   3842971, 172483, 34271, ?

5. Divide 500 by a quarter and add 50. How many have you got?

6. In the morning, a news vendor sold two copies of one magazine and five copies of a newspaper for a total of $15. In the afternoon, he sold five copies of the same magazine and two copies of the same newspaper for a total of $18.60. What is the cost of one newspaper and one magazine?

7. The following words are in a logical progression:

PLACEBOS, SECLUDED, SPECIFIC

Which one of the following comes next?

MAGAZINE, TOGETHER, CHIPMUNK, ANYWHERE, BARITONE

8. At the zoo the numbers of the animals' cages were:

LION	16
SEA LION	27
MONKEY	26
ANTELOPE	32

What is the number of the buffalo's cage?

9. A piece of land was up for sale at $50 per square yard. What will the cost be?

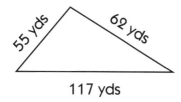

117 yds

10. At a holiday camp there were 38 holiday makers. There will be at least 19 people who are mutual friends, or at least 19 people who are mutual strangers. True or false?

11. WHAT IS THIS?

Take half of this,
and add one more.
Then triple that,
and add on four.
But just the same
result you'd see
if now you had added 23.

12. A man started a business with $2000 and increased his wealth by 50% every 3 years. How much did he possess after 18 years?

13. Deduct four thousand eleven hundred and a half from twelve thousand twelve hundred and twelve. What is the answer?

14. If you add the square of Tony's age to the age of Margaret, the sum is 62. If you add the square of Margaret's age to the age of Tony, the result is 176. What are Tony's and Margaret's ages?

15. Four burglars were being questioned by the police about a robbery.

"Jack did it," said Alan.
"George did it," said Jack.
"It wasn't me," said Sid.
"Jack is a liar if he said that I did it," said George.

Only one had spoken the truth. Who was the culprit?

Calculation and Logic

1. What letter is two to the left of the letter immediately to the right of the letter which is midway between the letter immediately to the right of the letter B and the letter immediately to the left of the letter H?

   A B C D E F G H

2. Tom, Dick, and Harry wish to share a certain sum of money among them. Tom gets $\frac{3}{5}$, Dick gets 0.35, and Harry gets $325. How much is the original sum of money?

3. Harry is a one-and-a-quarter times Dick's age, and Dick is one-and-a-quarter times Tom's age. Their combined ages total 122. How old are the three men?

4. 3 8 7 2 5   is to   7 5 8 3 2   as

   9 1 4 8 2   is to

   A. 18429   **B.** 13493   **C.** 24198   **D.** 49821   **E.** 42198

5. In a quiz show, the winner is allowed to pick four box numbers at random out of a total of ten boxes. Just four of the boxes contain a valuable prize, while six of the boxes contain something that is worthless. What are the chances that the contestant will be lucky enough to win all four of the valuable prizes?

6. Tom, Dick, and Harry have 84 among them. If Tom and Harry put theirs together, they have twice as many as Dick. If Dick and Harry put theirs together, they will have the same number as Tom. How many does each of them have?

7. Dallas, Texas, is 756 miles away from Detroit, Michigan. A nonstop train leaves Dallas traveling at 80 mph. Another nonstop train leaves Detroit at exactly the same time traveling at 90 mph. Which train will be farther from Dallas when they meet?

8. If $61 \rightarrow 55$
            $23 \rightarrow 21$
            $84 \rightarrow 76$

   What does $41 \rightarrow$?

9. How many revolutions must the largest cog make in order to bring the cogs back to their original positions?

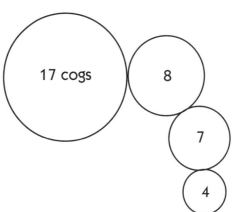

10. How many squares are there on an 8 × 8 square chessboard?

11. "Did you catch anything?" said Jill.

Her husband said, "A large fish. It weighed $\frac{6}{7}$ of its weight + $\frac{2}{3}$ of a pound."

What did the fish weigh?

12. Find the missing number.

```
7   6   5   16
9   14  11  25
13  26  17  ?
25  32  23  49
```

13. A said to B, "Here is my wallet. Give me the same amount of money as there is in the wallet." B counted the money and added to it the same amount. B said to A, "Give me as much as I have left and we will be all square." A said that he had $3.50 left. B said he had $3. How much did each possess at first?

14. Which number added to 100 and 164 will make them both perfect square numbers?

15. I knew an oldish lady in Dundee,
Whose age has its last digit "3."
The square of the first
Is her whole age reversed.
So what must the lady's age be?

Multidiscipline

1. Find the starting point and work from letter to adjoining letter, horizontally and vertically, but not diagonally, to spell out a twelve-letter word. You have to provide the missing letters.

R	A	A	
		M	I
A	I	D	C

2. If a man and a half can build a wall and a half in a day and a half, how many walls will twelve men build in 12 days?

3. What comes next in the sequence?

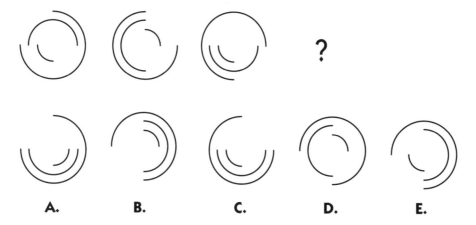

A.   **B.**   **C.**   **D.**   **E.**

4. Solve the anagram in parentheses to correctly complete the quotation by Robert E. Sherwood:

The trouble with me is I belong to a vanishing race. I'm one of the

(TALLEST NUCLEI).

5. What numbers should replace the question marks?

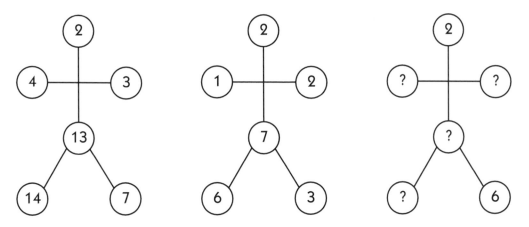

6. Which is the odd one out?

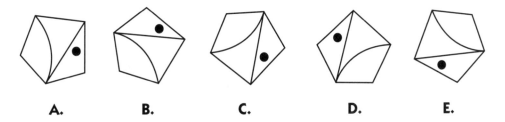

   A.   **B.**   **C.**   **D.**   **E.**

7. CHANGE (COAST) RESORT

Using the same logic as in the example above, what word is coded to appear in the parentheses below?

DRUDGE (_ _ _ _ _) UNBOLT

8. What number continues the sequence?

8573, 2961, 4857, 3296, ?

9. In a town of 14,500 people, a rich man gave away a total of $14,500. He wanted to give all of the males in the town a certain sum of money and all of the females $3.

Of the males, only half of them claimed their bonus. And of the females, only one-third claimed the money.

How much did he give each male?

10. A man is interrogating his five sons, one of whom has broken a pane of glass in the family greenhouse. Just three of the following statements is proved to be correct. Who broke the glass?

George: Phil broke the glass.
Bill: It was not me.
Al: It was not Ken.
Phil: George is lying.
Ken: Bill is telling the truth.

11.

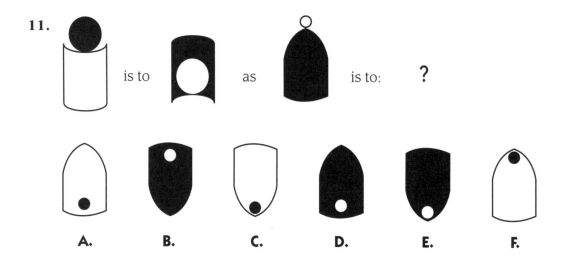

12. In a lottery of 6 winning numbers, how many tickets are there to include every set of 6 numbers out of 20?

13. What number should replace the question mark?

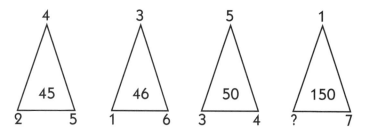

14. Give the next number in this series:

220, 200, 100, 80, 40, 20, ?

15. What number should replace the question mark to follow a definite rule?

$$14 + 55 \rightarrow 69$$
$$28 + 23 \rightarrow 60$$
$$22 + 31 \rightarrow 35$$
$$17 + 28 \rightarrow 99$$
$$41 + 27 \rightarrow ?$$

16. Which four-letter word can be placed at the begining of these six words to make six new words.

(_ _ _ _)

MADE
CUFF
RAIL
STAND
BASKET
WRITING

17. Find a nine-letter word by moving from letter to letter. Each letter can only be used once.

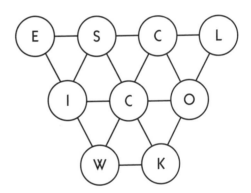

18. What element is also known as QUICKSILVER?

(a) LEAD
(b) COPPER
(c) MERCURY
(d) KRYPTON
(e) TIN

19. Going clockwise or counterclockwise, fill in the blanks to find the names of two flowers.

20. Which word means the same as MISSAL?

(a) PRAYER BOOK
(b) STONE PILLAR
(c) MESSAGE
(d) WEAPON
(e) MISTLETOE

Multidiscipline

1. What comes next in
the sequence?

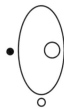  

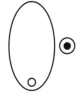    

A.   **B.**   **C.**   **D.**   **E.**

2. What number should replace the question mark?

36 (1312) 97
42 (106) 28
75 (?) 98

3. SAPPHIRE : BLUE

CARMINE :

   A. WHITE   **B.** PINK   **C.** BLACK   **D.** GREEN   **E.** RED

4. What number should replace the question mark?

5. Which day immediately follows the day three days before the day which immediately follows the day three days before Friday?

SUNDAY
MONDAY
TUESDAY
WEDNESDAY
THURSDAY
FRIDAY
SATURDAY

6. Which of the following is not an anagram of a type of vehicle?

ROT CART
AIR GRACE
CRAB LACE
DUST ARM
CUBAN MALE

7. What number should replace the question mark?

6	8	14	20
2	5	7	9
8	13	21	29
14	21	35	?

8. Go clockwise to find a ten-letter word. You must find the starting point and provide the missing letters. The word you are looking for starts and finishes with the same two letters.

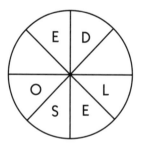

9. Two men run a race of 200 yards. Man A wins by 10 yards. Because of this, they decide to make things fairer for the next race by making Man A stand 10 yards behind the line, thereby giving Man B a 10-yard head start. They both run the second race at exactly the same speed as before. What is the result?

10.

 is to

as

 is to

A.   **B.**   **C.**   **D.**

11. Join two of the three-letter groups together to make a six-letter word which is a vegetable.

END - NEL - MAR - ROT - FEN - IVA

12. What word means the same as LIMBER?

(a) STRAINED
(b) LITHE
(c) DESTITUTE
(d) COMPETENCE
(e) LATENT

13. What kind of animal is a POCHARD?

(a) DUCK
(b) SALAMANDER
(c) GORILLA
(d) ANTELOPE

14. Place two of the three-letter groups together to make a six-letter word.

CUG - MAG - KOR - PIE - EAG - PER

15. $\dfrac{444 - 44}{4} = 100.$

Now find another way of arranging six 4s to equal 100 just by using any of the mathematical symbols (+, −, ×, ÷) plus brackets and parentheses but no decimals.

16. How many ways are there to travel from A to B following the arrows?

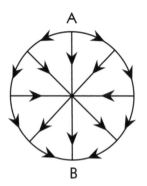

17. Find two one-word anagrams for

TRIBAL ACE

18. What number should replace the question mark?

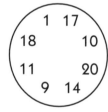 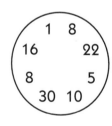 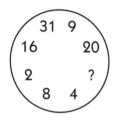

19. What number should replace the question mark?

20. Each line and symbol which appears in the four outer circles is transferred to the center circle according to these rules:

If a line or symbol occurs in the outer circles:
once, then it is transferred.
twice, then it is possibly transferred.
three times, then it is transferred.
four times, then it is not transferred.

Which of the circles A, B, C, D, or E shown below should appear at the center of the diagram above?

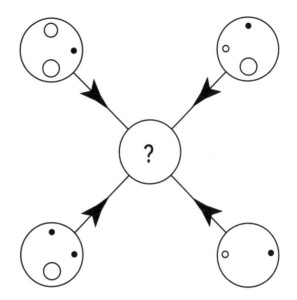

| A. | B. | C. | D. | E. |

Multidiscipline

1. What is the missing number?

15, 35, 23, 31, 31, ? , 39

2. With the aid of the two clues below, find two words that differ only by the omission of a single letter. For example: CRATER, CATER.

BEAT WITH/DISAPPOINT

3. Which is the odd one out?

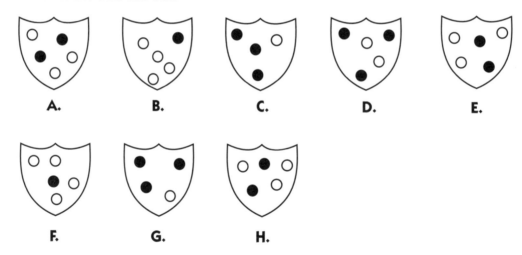

4. What number should replace the question mark?

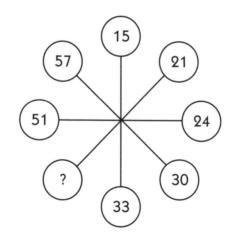

5. Arrange these words into three groups of two words each to find three words on the same theme.

AN, , PER, ROT, BE, PEP, CAR

6. Which circle should replace the question mark?

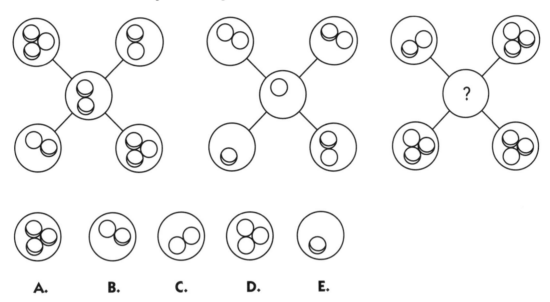

A. **B.** **C.** **D.** **E.**

7. What weight should be placed at the question mark for the scales to balance?

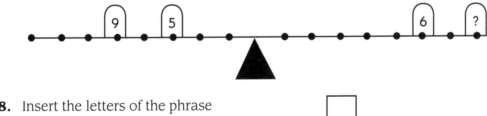

8. Insert the letters of the phrase WADED MY CAR into the blank spaces to find two connected words.

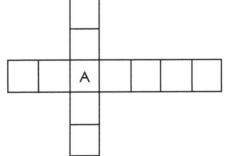

9. How many minutes is it before 12 noon if 84 minutes ago it was five times as many minutes past 9 AM as it is minutes before noon now?

10. Which is the odd one out?

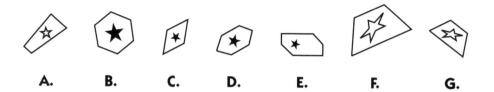

A.   B.   C.   D.   E.   F.   G.

Rebuses

A rebus is an arrangement of letters or symbols to represent a familiar word or phrase. Find the word or phrase in Questions 11–14.

11.

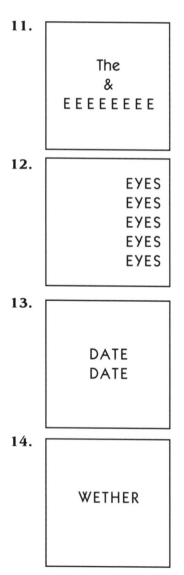

```
      The
       &
  E E E E E E E E
```

12.

```
            EYES
            EYES
            EYES
            EYES
            EYES
```

13.

```
    DATE
    DATE
```

14.

```
    WETHER
```

15. A man climbed a hill at 1½ miles an hour. Coming down, he went 4½ miles an hour. The whole trip took 6 hours. How many miles is it to the top of the hill?

16. What number should replace the question mark?

17	1	8	2
37	7	5	6
18	4	2	?
21	3	6	3
19	3	4	4

17. Starting from a corner square and spiraling to the center, fill in the missing letters to make a nine-letter word.

A		R
U	E	I
	L	L

18. Starting at a corner and spiraling to the center, find a nine-letter word.

P	I	H
I	O	C
S	T	A

19. Fill in the blanks to find two 8-letter words which are antonyms.

20. Each line and symbol which appears in the four outer circles is transferred to the center circle according to these rules:

If a line or symbol occurs in the outer circles:
   once, then it is transferred.
   twice, then it is possibly transferred.
   three times, then it is transferred.
   four times, then it is not transferred.

Which of the circles A, B, C, D or E shown below should appear at the center of the diagram above?

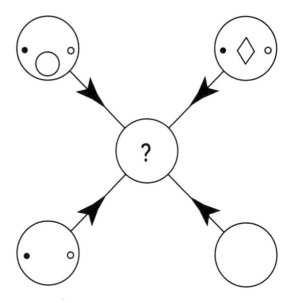

   A.   **B.**   **C.**   **D.**   **E.**

Multidiscipline

1. Which one of the following is not an anagram of HIPPOPOTAMUSES?

THIS POMPOUS APE
I'M A PET SHOP SOUP
SOAP PIPE MOUTHS
MASH UP OPPOSITE
PIE SPOUT MISHAP
IMPOSE PATHOS UP
OH! SOS! I'M A PUPPET
MISHAP OUTS POPE
OOPS! UP SHIPMATE

2. What logically is the missing number?

WET = 10
FINE = 11
HAIL = 9
HOT = 5
SNOW = ?

3. What comes next in the sequence?

A.   **B.**   **C.**   **D.**

4. Two of the three words below can be paired up to form an anagram of one word, which is a synonym of the word remaining. For example: LEG - MEEK – NET. The answer is GENTLE (MEEK).

LEAN - MUSIC - MALE

5. What number should replace the question mark?

6. What comes next in the sequence?

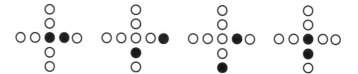

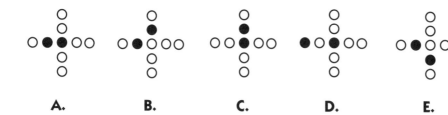

A.   **B.**   **C.**   **D.**   **E.**

7. What number comes next?

0, 1, 4, 9, 10, 13, 18, 19, ?

8. What number should replace the question mark?

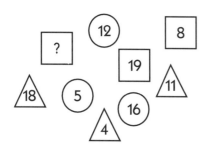

9. Which is the odd one out?

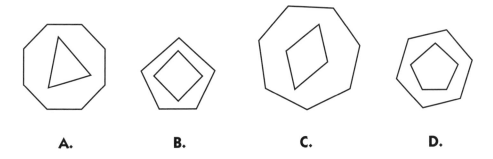

A. B. C. D.

10. Which two words that sound alike but are spelled differently mean:

DEMURE/REMAINED?

11. All the vowels have been omitted from this trite saying. Try to put them back.

NVRRG   WTHFL   PPLMG   HTNTK   NWTHD   FFRNC

12. Place these numbers in the small circles so that each set of 4 numbers on each circumference adds up to 60.

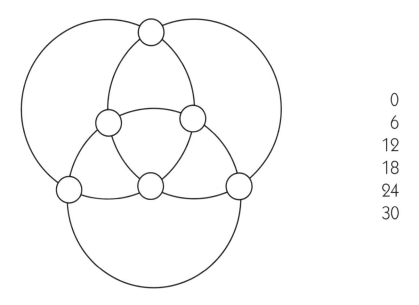

0
6
12
18
24
30

13. My watch was correct at midnight, but began to lose 12 minutes per hour. It now shows 1 o'clock in the morning, but stopped 10 hours ago. What time is it?

14. Find the value for x:

$$7 + 5 \div 2 + 6 \times 1 - 8 = x$$

15. What number should replace the question mark?

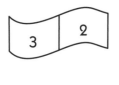  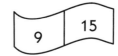

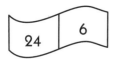 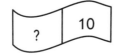

16. Find a twelve-letter word by moving from circle to circle. Each letter must only be used once.

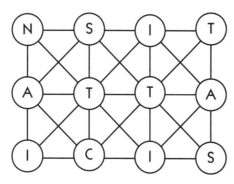

17. Place a three-letter word in front of these words to make new words.

TEST
TENT
(_ _ _) DUCT
SENT
FUSE
SIGN

18. All of the vowels have been omitted in this phrase. Can you figure out what the vowels are to complete it?

MRKSM NSNWH SHTSF RSTND WHTVR HHTSH CLLSH STRGT

19. Each of the nine squares in the grid marked 1A to 3C should incorporate all the lines and symbols which are shown in the squares of the same letter and number immediately above and to the left. For example, 1A should incorporate all the lines and symbols that are in 1 and C.

One of the squares is incorrect. Which one is it?

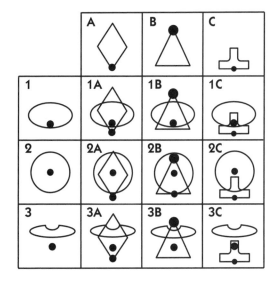

20. Change this recurring decimal into a fraction.

.19191919 . . .

Multidiscipline

1. What is the longest word that can be spelled out by moving from letter to adjacent letter horizontally, vertically, or diagonally and not repeating a letter?

F	R	A	C	I
Y	P	J	T	M
K	G	O	X	N
S	V	H	L	U
W	B	E	Q	D

2. Out of 100 people surveyed, 78 had an egg for breakfast, 82 had bread, 76 had bacon, and 88 had coffee. How many people, at least, must have had all four items—i.e., egg, bacon, toast, and coffee?

3. Which is the odd one out?

   A.　　　**B.**　　　**C.**　　　**D.**　　　**E.**

4. What number should replace the question mark?

5. Unscramble these four anagrammed words to find what they have in common.

   NOMAD, GRADE, SMILE, ASHEN

6. Insert the consonants below to complete the magic word grid on the right where all words read the same across and down. Use each consonant once.

	A		E	
A		O		E
	O		E	
E		E		
	E			

R   Z   S   D   R
T   N   C   D   C
N   T   D   T   T

7. What letter is three to the right of the letter immediately to the left of the letter two to the right of the letter immediately to the left of the letter E?

A B C D E F G H

8. Which circle should replace the question mark?

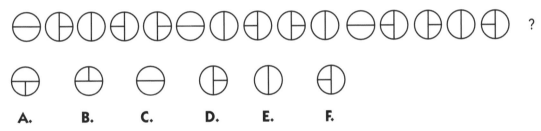

?

A.   **B.**   **C.**   **D.**   **E.**   **F.**

9. What is the missing number?

4827 : 2816
7526 : 4210
6974 : ?

10. Which is the odd one out?

    A.   **B.**   **C.**   **D.**   **E.**

11. We have been visited by aliens. Some have four eyes, some six eyes, some eight eyes, and some twelve eyes. There are an equal number of each type of alien. The total eyes in the room is 5130. How many aliens are there?

12. Each of the nine squares in the grid marked 1A to 3C should incorporate all the lines and symbols which are shown in the squares of the same letter and number immediately above and to the left. For example, 1A should incorporate all the lines and symbols that are in 1 and A.

One of the squares is incorrect. Which one is it?

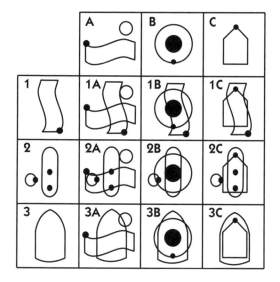

13. Replace the letters with numbers.

```
  E I G H T
  T H R E E
+   N I N E
  ─────────
T W E N T Y
```

Clue: R = 2G

14. Simplify

$7 - 2 \times 21 + 12 \div 4.$

15. What number should replace the question mark?

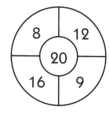 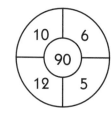 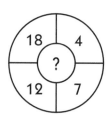

16. A ball is thrown into the air towards the person 50 yards away. What is the name given to the curve traveled by the ball?

17. In a relay race, the 1st runner of the team hands on the baton after having raced half the distance plus ½ mile. The second runner runs ⅓ of the remaining distance plus ⅓ mile. The third runner reaches the goal after having raced ¼ of the remaining distance plus ¼ mile. How long was the course?

18. What number should replace the question mark?

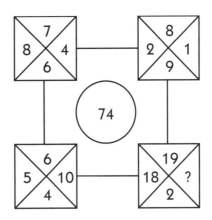

19. Find a twelve-letter phrase (5, 7) by moving from circle to circle. Each letter can only be used once.

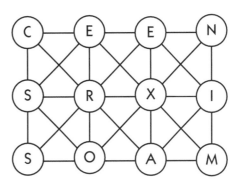

20. Going clockwise or counterclockwise, fill in the blanks to find a word.

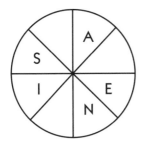

ANSWERS

Verbal

Test 1

1. ADMIRE, REASON, ONSIDE, DEFILE, LENGTH, THREAD
2. Firing on all cylinders.
3. OBLITERATE, CREATE
4. ARTIFICE
5. LIKE FATHER LIKE SON
6. GRACIOUS, CORDIAL
7. BALL
8. ACACIA
9. BLUSHING
10. HOUSE
11. WIGGLE
12. SUGGESTIVE
13. WASHROOM
14. MAJESTIC, STRIKING
15. PAPUA NEW GUINEA

Test 2

1. LOQUACIOUS
2. END. ENDOWED, ENDEAR, ENDLESS, ENDLONG, ENDANGER.
3. MISCOMPREHENSION
4. ENCIPHER
5. GOWN. All the words in the left-hand column can now be prefixed with NIGHT and all the words in the right-hand column can now be prefixed with DAY.
6. NICHE, PLACE
7. Sell like hot cakes.
8. MALADROIT, DEXTROUS
9. CAPUCHIN
10. (c) CONVOCATION
11. MONKEY
12. FISH
13. Anyone who thinks there is some good in everyone hasn't interviewed enough people.
14. ORANGUTAN
15. PINNACLE

Test 3

1. NECESSARY, SUPERFLUOUS
2. PARTISAN, OPPONENT
3. (c) SALAMANDER
4. EVIL OLIVE
5. MICROWAVE
6. RIPE/PEAR, CODE/DEER, LAST/STAR, OVAL/ALLY. Eight-letter word: PEDESTAL
7. RUDDER
8. (d) AFFIRMATION
9. CHIVES
10. SOUBRETTE
11. Society is threatened less by the fat around the middle than it is menaced by the fat between the ears.
12. DULLNESS, RADIANCE
13. They are all aquatic creatures: CARP, CRAB, DACE, CHUB, NEWT
14. BATHYSCOPE
15. FENCING, CRICKET

Test 4

1. SABTL = BLAST
2. BANAL
3. SCUBA DIVER
4. Chance favors the prepared mind.
5. RATIONAL, SENSIBLE
6. FAULTY, IMPERFECT
7. PLAUSIBLE
8. The world gets better every day then worse again in the evening.
9. OBSTINATE, DOGGED
10. (a) A SHELL
11. INVECTIVE, SECRETION
12. (e) WHITE
13. MEDIOCRE, ORDINARY
14. PUSSYCAT
15. UMBRELLA

Test 5

1. CONSORT
2. C(HERO)KEE
3. GRATE

---

4. XYZ = TOP. TOPPLE, UTOPIA, ESTOPS, LAPTOP
5. ROCHESTER: FIR, TOO, ARC, ASH, PIE, WAS, PAT, RUE, BAR
6. EMERALD, AMETHYST, TOPAZ
7. BREAD, PIZZA, STEAK, BACON, HONEY
8. SECOND
9. TREADMILL
10. FLOUNDER
11. ASSASSINS
12. IMPUDENT, CONTRARY
13. WHIRLWINDS
14. Once you can open a can of worms, the only way to recan them is to use a longer can.
15. CANDLEWICK

Visual

Test 1

1. D. The figure rotates 90° clockwise at each stage and a different section is shaded in turn.
2. E. Triangles turn to circles and vice versa, and white figures turn to black and vice versa.
3. E. In all the others, the triangle is in the largest rectangle, the shield is in the smallest rectangle (the square), and the other figure is in the second largest rectangle.
4. B. The bottom horizontal line of the first figure disappears and the bottom right vertical line in the second figure is added.
5. C. In all the others, the pattern on the outside is repeated in the center.
6. D. Matching triangles in the same position of the first three hexagons cancel each other out. If all three triangles match, then the position in the fourth hexagon is a blank.
7. B. Each of the three shapes, even though they are of different sizes, appears black, white, and striped.
8. B. At each stage the top left-hand line is moving through half the length of one side clockwise.
9. C. E and G are a mirror image, as are A and F, and B and D.

10. A. The center geometric shape adds on an additional side. All dots change from white to black, and vice versa.

11. B. The large half-circle moves from right to top to left to bottom. The medium half-circle alternates from left to right. The small half-circle moves from bottom to right to top to left. The center dot alternates between appearing and disappearing.

12. E. A is the same as G. F is the same as B. C is the same as D.

13. D. When two figures touch, they disappear at the next stage and are replaced by two different figures.

14. 20. $4 + 3 + 6 + 5 + 2 = 20$. The opposite sides of a die always add to 7.

15. $6\frac{3}{7}$ square units

Test 2

1. E. The diamond rotates 90°. The square goes inside the diamond. The semicircle rotates 180° and moves to the top.

2. B. There are two alternate sequences in which a larger circle is added at each stage.

3. B. A is the same as D. C is the same as E.

4. D. The dot in the top left-hand quarter moves backward and forward between two corners, as does the dot in the bottom left-hand quarter. The dot in the top right-hand quarter moves one corner counterclockwise at each stage and the dot in the bottom right-hand quarter moves one corner clockwise.

5. F. This way, each row and column contains four white stars and five black stars.

6. D. Working counterclockwise, the large circle is losing one quarter of its circumference at each stage. The small circle is increasing by a quarter of its circumference at each counterclockwise stage.

7. E. It contains a circle in a triangle, a black dot in a diamond, a white circle in a black circle, and a black triangle in a circle.

8. E. All the others consist of three identical figures when rotated. E has only two figures which when rotated are identical.

9. A

10. B. The symbols change position as in the example.

11. E. A is the same as B rotated. C is the same as G rotated. D is the same as F rotated.

12. A. R + S = T; X + Y = Z. But similar symbols disappear.

13. E

14. E. All the others have a matching circle rotated 90° (B-G, C-D, E-F).

15. 318°.

A. $\frac{360°}{4} = 90°$ 90°

B. $\frac{360}{5} = 72°$ $180° - 72° = 108°$

C. $\frac{360}{6} = 60°$ $180° - 60° = 120°$

    $90° + 108° + 120° = 318°$

Test 3

1. C. In all the others, the black circle is directly connected to three white circles.

2. C. The bottom right-hand quarter increases in size and becomes the main figure. The two components that previously made up the main figure go inside the new main figure.

3. 17

4. H. In all the others, the figure on the outside is repeated in the middle.

5. A. The third pentagon of each row and column contains only lines that appear twice in the same position in the first two pentagons. However, these lines change from straight to curved and vice versa.

6. H. All the others have a mirror-image pairing.

7. D. Then the dot appears in the

diamond and one circle.

8. C

9. D. A is the same as F. B is the same as E. C is the same as G.

10. A

11. C

12. D

13. 2A

14. +. The order of the symbols is: x + o x ≈ □

15. B

Numerical
Test 1

1. 41. $7 \times 8 - 15 = 41$.

2. 4763. Reverse the previous number and add 1 to the same digit each time.

3. 8. In opposite segments, alternate pairs of digits total the same. $19 + 3 = 14 + 8$.

4. 9598. $5217 + 4381 = 9598$.

5. 1. $3 \times 8 - 6 = 18$. Similarly, $6 \times 9 - 5 = 49$.

6.
3824	116	17
4968	144	18
7519	130	13

$32 + 84 = 116$, $16 + 1 = 17$.

7. 12. All the other numbers are a quarter of or four times another number: 18/72, 5/20, 9/36, 4/16.

8. $2\frac{1}{2}$ kg.

9. 22
$(7 \times 8) - (5 \times 4) = 36$
$(9 \times 3) - (5 \times 2) = 17$
$(8 \times 5) - (6 \times 3) = 22$

10. $\frac{166}{999}$.

$1000x = 166.166166\ldots$
$1x = .166166\ldots$
$999x = 166$

$x = \frac{166}{999}$

11. 10. Each side adds up to 50.

12. 42. $(5 \times 8) - 7 = 33.$
$(6 \times 7) - 6 = 36.$
$(7 \times 5) - 4 = 31.$
$(8 \times 7) - 14 = 42.$

13. 8. Add the top row of numbers to the second row to obtain the bottom row; i.e., 42986 + 38795 = 81781.

14. 15. Add 1, 2, 3, and repeat.

15. 68. $(8 \times 9) - 3 = 69.$
$(7 \times 5) - 6 = 29.$
$(4 \times 7) - 9 = 19.$
$(9 \times 8) - 4 = 68.$

𝒯est 2

1. 28

2. 7

3. 9. $39^2 = 1521.$
Similarly, $76^2 = 5776.$

4. 12. The outer number added to its two connected numbers always totals 20. For example: 3 + 7 + 10 = 20, 7 + 4 + 9 = 20, etc.

5. 16. 7 + 2 – 2 + 9 = 16.

6. 2. Each row and column alternate sums of 19 and 17.

7. 216. The number in the center of each figure is the cube of the number of sides of the figure.

8. 27. The total of three numbers is 72 (24 x 3). The total of two numbers is 45 ($22\frac{1}{2}$ x 2). The third number must be 27 (72 – 45).

9. 60. 60 + 9(15%) = 69.

10. 40. There are 2 series: (+ $3\frac{1}{4}$) 27, $30\frac{1}{4}$, $33\frac{1}{2}$, $36\frac{3}{4}$, 40
($-3\frac{1}{4}$) 27, $23\frac{3}{4}$, $20\frac{1}{2}$, $17\frac{1}{4}$, 14

11. 4. (39 – 3) ÷ 4 = 9.
(54 – 6) ÷ 8 = 6.
(45 – 36) ÷ 9 = 1.
(35 – 7) ÷ 7 = 4.

12. 92. 12 + 6 + 7 = 25. Reverse = 52.
17 + 9 + 9 = 35. Reverse = 53.
7 + 4 + 8 = 19. Reverse = 91.
11 + 13 + 5 = 29. Reverse = 92.

13. 41. The first column has even numbers starting at 26. The second column has odd numbers starting at 27. The third column

has prime numbers starting at 29. The fourth column has square numbers starting at 25.

14. D. It is a perfect cube (3^3). The rest are all perfect squares.

15. 30.
$$\frac{7 \times 4 \times 3}{6} = 14.$$
$$\frac{9 \times 2 \times 6}{6} = 18.$$
$$\frac{12 \times 2 \times 4}{6} = 16.$$
$$\frac{9 \times 4 \times 5}{6} = 30.$$

𝒯est 3

1. 25746. Multiply the previous number by 8 and add 2 each time.

2. 31. Start at 1 and work clockwise to each segment, adding 3, 6, 9, 12, 15, 18.

3. 9. Look across to same sections in each of the three figures: 4, 6, 8 (increase by 2); 9, 7, 5 (reduce by 2); 8, 5, 2 (reduce by 3); 1, 5, 9 (increase by 4).

4. 9. Looking across, rows having two numbers total 14, rows having three numbers total 18, and rows having four numbers total 22.

5. 210. 7 x 6 x 1 x 5 = 210.

6. 11. $\dfrac{19 + 25}{4} = 11$

7. 5827 in the top and 1826 in the bottom. Each of the other numbers has anagram pairings top and bottom: 4829/2894, 7136/6731, 6483/8346, 9514/1459, 6127/7621, 3816/6813.

8. 18. 16 x 9 = 8x
144 = 8x
18 = x

9. 173. 87 + 86 = 173.

10. 46. Beginning at 17, go across the row and then follow the direction of the arrows alternating between +9 and –5.

11. LQ

12. 19

	7	12	9
+6	13	18	15
–2	11	16	13
+6	17	22	19

13. 2. Subtract the sum of the even numbers from the sum of the odd numbers.
7 + 9 = 16   9 + 3 = 12
2 + 4 = 6   4 + 6 = 10
16 – 6 = 10   12 – 10 = 2

14. 11. $(42 \div 7) + 6 = 12.$
$(91 \div 13) + 4 = 11.$
$(88 \div 11) + 5 = 13.$
$(27 \div 9) + 8 = 11.$

15. 49. Add the sum of the two digits in each box to the number to get the number in the next box. For example, 1 + 6 = 7; 7 + 16 = 23.

𝒯est 4

1. 212. 7 x 3 = 21, 1 + 1 = 2.

2. 9. Looking across each row of numbers, the bottom row totals 5, the fourth row totals 6, the third row totals 7, and the second row totals 8. Therefore, the top row should total 9.

3. 41. These are the prime numbers from 17 to 41.

4. 32. Multiply by 3 and add 2 to obtain the pairings; so, 10 x 3 = 30; 30 + 2 = 32.
The other such pairs are: 3/11, 7/23, 20/62, 2/8, 16/50, and 15/47.

5. 9. 16 x 6 = 96. Similarly, 29 x 3 = 87 and 15 x 5 = 75.

6.
A	B	C	D	E
2	4	3	7	11
10	5	13	9	7
22	23	17	19	18
36	39	40	41	40

A + C = B in the row below.
C + D = A in the row below.
A + E = C in the row below.
B + C = E in the row below.
A + D = D in the row below.

7. ⅙

8. 802/1125. 1000x = 712.888888...

$$x = \quad .712888...$$

$$999x = 712.176$$

$$999000x = 712176$$

$$x = \frac{712176}{999000}$$

$$x = \frac{802}{1125}$$

9. 99. There are 2 series: (+4¼)
82, 86¼, 90½, 93¾, 99

(–4¼) 82, 77¾, 73½, 69¼

10. 4

11. 135°. $\frac{360°}{8} = 45°$

$$180° - 45° = 135°.$$

12. 28. (6 + 7) × 4 = 52.

(8 + 5) × 3 = 39.

(4 + 3) × 8 = 56.

(5 + 2) × 4 = 28.

13. 10879. Add the number to the reverse of its digits. For example: 163 + 361 = 524, etc.

14. 14.

LH	RH
5 × 14 = 70	3 × 9 = 27
1 × 10 = 10	6 × 8 = 48
‾‾80	1 × 5 = 5
	‾‾80

15. LM

Test 5

1. 110. The sequence progresses – 1 × 2, – 2 × 2, – 3 × 2, – 4 × 2, – 5 × 2. So, 60 – 5 = 55; 55 × 2 = 110.

2. 19. 3 × 9 = 27; 27 – 8 = 19.

3. 8429. In all the others, the last two digits multiplied together is equal to the first two digits.

4. 1716. 39 × 44.

5. 3. 6 × 7 = 42, 7 × 2 = 14; 42 ÷ 14 = 3.

6. 16. There are two alternate sequences that increase by 2 and 5, respectively, i.e., 1, 3, 5, 7 and 1, 6, 11, 16.

7. 32. 4 – 1 = 3 and 9 – 7 = 2.

8. 130. +18, +20, +22, +24.

9. 132. $7 + 2^3 = 15.$

$$7 + 3^3 = 34.$$

$$7 + 4^3 = 71.$$

$$7 + 5^3 = 132.$$

10. 171.

1st CIRCLE	2nd CIRCLE	3rd CIRCLE
17 × 4 = 68	7 × 6 = 42	21 × 9 = 189
13 × 4 = 52	11 × 6 = 66	14 × 9 = 126
19 × 4 = 76	16 × 6 = 96	19 × 9 = 171

11. 12.

10 + 11 + 13 + 5 = 39; 39 ÷ 3 = 13

17 + 5 + 9 + 17 = 48; 48 ÷ 3 = 16

19 + 6 + 7 + 10 = 42; 42 ÷ 3 = 14

9 + 15 + 6 + 6 = 36; 36 ÷ 3 = 12

12. 4. $4^2 + 3^2 = 25$

$$6^2 + 2^2 = 40$$

$$7^2 + 5^2 = 74$$

$$5^2 + 4^2 = 41$$

13. 831. The number sequence 1724683 repeats.

14. 1.

$$\frac{17}{19} \div \frac{68}{38} \div \frac{16}{32} = \frac{17}{19} \times \frac{38}{68} \times \frac{32}{16} = 1.$$

15.

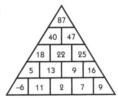

Calculation and Logic
Test 1

1. G

2. 37 minutes

3. Jim 28, Alf 42, Sid 63. 28 + 14 = 42, 42 + 21 = 63.

4. TRUCULENT. Each word starts with the letter in the alphabet following the last letter of the previous word. The length of the words increases by one each time.

5. Lemon = 60¢, orange = 80¢

6. 11 PM

7. 29 apples into 23 bags. 667 is the product of two prime numbers, 23 and 29. The smaller of these two numbers is the number of bags, as you wish to use the smallest number of bags possible.

8. ⅘

9. $C = \frac{9}{5}F + 32$

$$F = \frac{5}{9}(C - 32)$$

10. 80. $\frac{60 \times 20}{15} = 80.$

16 slices = 15 cuts

11. 25 ft × 25 ft. 15 ft × 15 ft.

12. 107. 99 – (4 × 9) = 63.

63 + (4 × 11) = 107.

13. C. It has five right angles. The others have four right angles.

14. 210 days. 5 × 6 × 7.

15. Find the center point S/N + E/W of the six dots. The answer is C4.

Test 2

1. Bill.

2. B. They are the letters K, L, M, and N on their side. So O is the next one.

3. BRIEF.

1 3   2 (1 2 3 4 5)   5   4

BIKER (BRIEF) RIFLE

4. 1 minute 12 seconds:

$$\frac{(1.25 + 0.25) \times 60}{75} \quad \frac{1.5 \times 60}{75}$$

= 1.2 minutes or 1 minute 12 seconds

5. 168 lbs. 75% × 168 = 126; 126 + 42 = 168.

6. Originally, Frasier had sixteen, Nils had eight, and Daphne had four. Then Daphne lost one, which meant she had three. She gave two to Frasier and one to Nils. This meant Frasier had eighteen and Nils had nine.

7. 10:00. The big hand moves two back at each stage and the small hand moves three forward.

8. Say that the kennel costs $k and the dog $d.

Then

$k = \frac{1}{3}(k + d + 5)$

$d = \frac{3}{4}(d + k - 5)$

Then

$2k - d = 5$ and

$3k - d = 15$.

so $k = 10$ and $d = 15$.

The dog costs $15 and the kennel costs $10.

9. 441 sq ft and 49 sq ft

10. One person had a piece on a plate.

11. 2147
2147
+418
————
4712

12. 54 years

13. Alice is 16, Barbara is 60, and Chloe is 80.

14. 4¾ kg.

LH	RH
4 kg × 4 = 16	6 kg × 2 = 12
5 kg × 3 = $\frac{15}{31}$	4¾ × 4 = $\frac{19}{31}$

15. 15 $(2^4 - 1)$

Test **3**

1. 21

2. 4 minutes

$\frac{1}{4.5} + \frac{1}{12} - \frac{1}{18} = .25$

$\frac{1}{.25} = 4$

3. Five; one of each in brown, blue, gray, green, and black.

4. The second option:

First option ($2000 increase after 12 months)

First year: $20,000 + $20,000 = $40,000

Second year: $21,000 + $21,000 = $42,000

Second option ($500 increase after 6 months)

First year: $20,000 + $20,500 = $40,500

Second year: $21,000 + $21,500 = $42,500

5. King of Hearts

6. Seventy-three people paid $39.

7. There are 13 lions and 17 eagles.

8. WEDNESDAY

9. 64. Question 1: No. 42 to 82.

Question 2: Yes. 44 – 48 – 52 – 56 – 60 – 68 – 72 – 76 – 80.

Question 3: Yes. 64.

10. They were playing pool in the club house.

11. 729. Statement 1 is a lie. The only square and cube number between 99 and 999 whose first and last digits are 5, 7, or 9 is 729.

12. 2519

13. Arthur would take 60 days. Bert would take 40 days.

14. 4027
  × 2
————
8054

15. $3456

Test **4**

1.

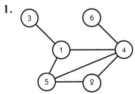

2. 39 socks. If he takes out 37 socks, although it's a long shot, they could be all blue and red. To be 100% certain that he has a pair of gray socks, he must take out two more.

3. 37.5 minutes

$\frac{50 \times 24}{32}$

4. 1243. Reverse the digits and drop the largest number each time.

5. 2050

6. Newspaper $1.80, magazine $3.00

7. TOGETHER: pl**A**ce**B**os

se**C**lu**D**ed

sp**E**ci**F**ic

to**G**et**H**er

8. 29. A vowel = 3, a consonant = 5.

9. The land doesn't exist. For a triangle to exist, the two smaller sides must be longer than the third side. It is an impossible triangle.

10. True. There must be one or the other.

11. 32. Say this is x,

Then, $3(\frac{1}{2}x + 1) + 4 = x + 23$

$x = 32$.

12. $22,781.25

13. 8111½

14. Tony is 7 years old. Margaret is 13 years old.

15.

Guilty	Truth spoken by
Jack	Alan, Sid, and George
George	Jack and Sid
Alan	Sid and George
Sid	George alone

So SID was the culprit.

Test **5**

1. D

2. $6500

3. Tom is 32, Dick is 40, and Harry is 50.

4. E. 42198

A	B	C	D	E
9	1	4	8	2
C	E	B	A	D
4	2	1	9	8

5. One chance in 210.

6. Tom has 42, Dick has 28, and Harry has 14.

7. No calculations are necessary. Obviously they will be both the same distance from Dallas when they meet, and they will both be the same distance from Detroit!

8. The number on the left is in base 9, and the number on the right is in base 10.

$41 \rightarrow 37$

9. 56. $8 \times 7 = 56$

10. 204.

$1^2, 2^2, 3^2, 4^2, 5^2, 6^2, 7^2, 8^2$

$1 + 4 + 9 + 16 + 25 + 36 + 49 + 64$

11. 4⅔ lb. ⅔ of a pound plus ⁶⁄₇ of its weight = complete weight. Hence, ⅔ of a pound equals ¹⁄₇ of its weight. So it weighs 7 x ²⁄₃ lb.

12. 36 (6²). The first column are odd numbers, the second column are even numbers, the third are prime numbers, and the fourth are square numbers.

13. A had $2.50. B had $4.

14. 125. If you add 125 to 100 and to 164, you get two square numbers, 225 and 289, the squares of 15 and 17.

15. Say the first digit of her age is x. Then her age in years is 10x + 3; its reverse is 30 + x. Then x = 30 + x. Hence x = 6. Her age is 63 years.

Multidiscipline

Test **1**

1. DIAGRAMMATIC

2. 96 walls. At this rate a man will build two-thirds of a wall in one day.

Therefore, 1 man = ²⁄₃ wall in 1 day

12 men = ²⁴⁄₃ (8) wall in 1 day.

Therefore, 12 men = 8 x 12 (96) walls in 12 days.

3. B. The outer arc moves 90° clockwise at each stage, the middle arc moves 90° counter-clockwise, and the inner arc moves 180°.

4. INTELLECTUALS

5.

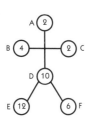

F − B = C

B + C + F = E

E/F = A

A x C + F = D

6. A. The rest are the same figure rotated.

7. DOUBT

1 3	(1 2 3 4 5)	4 2 5
DRUDGE	DOUBT	UNBOLT

8. 1485. The numbers 857329614 are being repeated in the same sequence.

9. $2.

Male: ½ x $2 = $1.

Female: ⅓ x $3 = $1.

10. Ken. This means that the three statements by Bill, Phil, and Ken are true.

11. C. The circle moves to the bottom of the main figure with black/white reversal.

12. 38,760.

13. 10. $2^2 + 5^2 + 4^2 = 45$.

$1^2 + 6^2 + 3^2 = 46$.

$3^2 + 4^2 + 5^2 = 50$.

$7^2 + 1^2 + 10^2 = 150$.

14. 10. −20, x ½, −20, x ½, −20, x ½

15. 113. Reverse the digits to the right of the plus sign.

16. HAND

17. CLOCKWISE

18. (C) MERCURY

19. ABUTILON, ACANTHUS

20. (a) PRAYER BOOK

Test **2**

1. C. The black dot is moving left to right at each stage, the white circle moves back and forth inside the ellipse, the small white dot moves inside and then outside the ellipse at each stage.

2. 1316. 5 + 8 = 13, 7 + 9 = 16.

3. E. RED.

4. 63. Start at 1 and jump clockwise to alternate segments while adding 2, 4, 8, 16, 32, 64 in turn.

5. MONDAY

6. DUST ARM = MUSTARD. The vehicles are TRACTOR (ROT CART), CARRIAGE (AIR GRACE), CABLE CAR (CRAB LACE), AMBULANCE (CUBAN MALE).

7. 49. Looking across each row and down each column, the first two numbers added together total the third number, and the first and third numbers added together total the fourth number.

8. MEDDLESOME

9. Man A again wins. We know from the first race that Man A runs 200 yards at the same time that Man B runs 190 yards. Therefore, it follows that as Man A starts 10 yards behind the line, the men will be dead even at 10 yards short of the winning line. As Man A is the faster runner, he goes on to overtake Man B in the last 10 yards and win the race.

10. B. The triangle folds into the hexagon and changes from white to black.

11. FENNEL

12. (b) LITHE

13. (a) DUCK

14. MAGPIE

15. 4 x [(4 x 4) + 4 + 4] + 4

16. 17

17. CALIBRATE and BACTERIAL

18. 10. All numbers in each circle total 100.

19. 83. 14 + 5 (= 1 + 4) = 19.

19 + 10 (= 1 + 9) = 29.

29 + 11 (= 2 + 9) = 40.

40 + 4 (= 4 + 0) = 44.

44 + 8 (= 4 + 4) = 52.

52 + 7 (= 5 + 2) = 59.

59 + 14 (= 5 + 9) = 73.

73 + 10 (= 7 + 3) = 83.

83 + 11 (= 8 + 3) = 94.

20. D

Test **3**

1. 27. There are two alternate sequences, +8 and −4.

2. FLAIL/FAIL

3. D. The only one with the combination of three black and two white. The rest have at least one matching pair. For example: A, E, and H have two black/three white.

4. 39. Start at 15 and, working clockwise, add the digits of the previous number to that number to obtain the next number.

5. BEAN, PEPPER, CARROT

6. A. The inner circle shows the difference in striped vs. plain circles in the outer circles. There are three more striped circles than plain circles in the four surrounding figures.

7. 3.

$5 \times 9 = 45$ $6 \times 6 = 36$

$3 \times 5 = \underline{15}$ $3 \times 8 = \underline{24}$
　　　　60　　　　　　　60

8. ACADEMY AWARD

9. 16 minutes

10. C. In all the others, black stars are in six-sided figures and white stars in four-sided figures.

11. THE ANDES

12. EYES RIGHT

13. DOUBLE DATE

14. A BAD SPELL OF WEATHER

15. 6¾ miles.

$$\frac{6\frac{3}{4}}{1\frac{1}{2}} + \frac{6\frac{3}{4}}{4\frac{1}{2}} = 6 \text{ hours}$$

16. 7.

$$\frac{17-1}{8} = 2 \quad \frac{37-7}{5} = 6$$

$$\frac{18-4}{2} = 7 \quad \frac{21-3}{6} = 3 \quad \frac{19-3}{4} = 4$$

17. QUADRILLE

18. PISTACHIO

19. DIMINISH, INCREASE

20. A

𝒯est 4

1. PIE SPOUT MISHAP

2. 7. It is the number of straight lines in each word.

3. B. The bottom square rotates 45° clockwise at each stage.

4. MALE MASCULINE

5. 17. Start at 2 and, working clockwise, jump three spaces each time adding 3.

6. A. One black dot moves down and back up after reaching the bottom at each stage. The other moves right at each stage then

back left upon reaching the end.

7. 22. Add 1, 3, and 5, and then repeat.

8. 6. This way, the sum of the numbers in the same shape totals 33.

9. B. The total number of sides in each of the other pairs of figures adds up to 11.

10. STAID/STAYED

11. Never argue with a fool. People might not know the difference.

12.

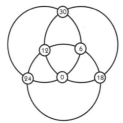

Other answers are possible.

13. 4:45 AM.

14. 7½. 7 + (2½) + (6) − 8 = 7½. Multiplication and division come before addition and subtraction.

15. 30. 2 + 3 = 5, 5 + 4 = 9, 9 + 15 = 24, 24 + 6 = 30.

16. STATISTICIAN

17. CON

18. A marksman is one who shoots first and whatever he hits he calls his target.

19. 2B

20. ¹⁹⁄₉₉.

100x = 19.191919…

x = .191919…

99x = 19

x = ¹⁹⁄₉₉.

𝒯est 5

1. VOLUNTARY

2. 24. Add the four percentages together, 78 + 82 + 76 + 88 = 324.

This leaves three items among 100 people and 24 people left over with all four items.

3. C. It rotates clockwise, the others rotate counterclockwise.

4. 3. The two left-hand numbers total the same as the three right-hand numbers, i.e., 7 + 6 = 13 and 9 + 1 + 3 = 13.

5. DAMON, EDGAR, MILES, SHANE

6.　　C A D E T
　　　　A D O R E
　　　　D O Z E N
　　　　E R E C T
　　　　T E N T S

7. H

8. C. Divide the circles into groups of four. In each group, the circle originally on the far left is moving one place to the right.

9. 2463. 6 × 4 = 24, 9 × 7 = 63.

10. B. In all the others, the five symbols are in the same order.

11. 171. 4 + 6 + 8 + 12 = 30 eyes. 5130 ÷ 30 = 171.

12. 2B

13.　　85291
　　　　19488
　　　+ 3538
　　───────
　　　108317

14. −32. 7 − (42) + (12 × 4) = −32.

15. 188. (8 × 16) − (12 × 9) = 20

(10 × 12) − (6 × 5) = 90

(18 × 12) − (4 × 7) = 188

16. PARABOLA

17. 3 miles. 1st: 1½ + ½ = 2

2nd: ⅓ + ⅓ = ⅔

3rd: ¹⁄₁₂ + ¼ = ⅓

18. 2. (7 × 6) + (8 × 4) = 74

(8 × 9) + (2 × 1) = 74

(6 × 4) + (5 × 10) = 74

(19 × 2) + (18 × 2) = 74

19. CROSS EXAMINE

20. MISTAKEN